The Beauty and G

A Masonic Devotional

by Walter William Melnyk, 32°, KT

Dedicated to
The Academy of Masonic Knowledge
of the Grand Lodge of Pennsylvania
Free & Accepted Masons

Graphics reproduced with permission from
The Grand Lodge of Ancient Free and Accepted Masons
of North Carolina, and
The Masonic Lodge of Education

Common Gavel Press

ISBN: 1449514685
EAN-13: 9781449514686

Author's Email
william.melnyk@verizon.net

Preface

It is commonly recognized that Freemasonry, while not being a religion, is spiritual in outlook. While this is accepted in the abstract, there has been little if anything of a spiritual nature provided for the individual Freemason who is seeking spiritual growth within the context of his Craft membership. The Working Tools of a Freemason are powerful symbols which may serve as steps in a spiritual journey toward maturity as an ethical and moral man. Author and editor Jonathan Black has observed, in his preface to Robert Lomas' book *The Secret Science of Masonic Initiation*,[1] that "the rites and symbols of Freemasonry are intended to awake, perhaps gently and over time, sometimes suddenly and decisively, any spiritual curiosity about esoteric mysteries that lies inside the individual, however deep, however dormant."

The purpose of this small booklet is to encourage Freemasons, through daily meditation upon the inner meanings of their symbolic Working Tools, to awaken within themselves the esoteric heart of Freemasonry, the spirituality of "making good men better." It is similar to devotional books found in various religions, not because Freemasonry is itself a religion, but because human spirituality is the same the world over, transcending the religious boundaries that separate us. In the spirituality of Freemasonry, one finds the foundation of what it means to be human, apart from the constricting and alienating dogmas of religious organizations. Still, the Freemason will find in this book nothing that is derogatory to his own religion, morals, or the laws of his community.

The book is designed to be used as a daily devotional guide through a weekly cycle, with a Masonic Working Tool assigned for each day.

Sunday is represented by the Compasses, which in many Masonic jurisdictions is not mentioned as a Working Tool of any one Degree and therefore applies to all Freemasons. It is a tool of preparation for the journey, through the disciplines of self-discovery and self-control.

Monday and Tuesday present the Tools of an Entered Apprentice Mason, and represent the first steps in the spiritual journey: those of personal growth. The Twenty-four Inch Gauge on Monday teaches lessons of stewardship of time, talents, and treasure. The Common Gavel on Tuesday inspires an understanding of personal conversion.

The Tools of a Fellowcraft Mason appear Wednesday through Friday, as the Freemason moves from personal growth to growth in community. Wednesday is the Plumb, which teaches integrity. On Thursday the Level reminds us of the ideal of equality. Friday brings the Square, which encourages us to meditate upon fairness.

On Saturday the Trowel of the Master Mason teaches us about the final integration of all steps in the journey, which is Brotherly Love and Affection.

And then on Sunday the journey begins anew, for spiritual growth is a never-ending spiral of learning and advancement.

Each day is divided into three equal parts, inspired by the Officers of the Craft Lodge and the concomitant journey of the Sun across the sky: Morning, as the Sun rises in the East to open and rule the day; Noon, as the Sun attains High Meridian, the beauty and glory of the day; and Evening, as the Sun sets in the West to close the day.

Each of these sections contains an opening prayer, a meditation based upon the Working Tool for the day, suggestions for Masonic action, and a closing prayer of intercession on behalf of one's Brethren and the world.

Additional benefit may be obtained by keeping a daily journal in which to record personal responses and observations. All this under the jurisdiction of the Great Architect of the Universe, who creates us, who loves us, and who ever inspires us to become better than we are.

Walter William Melnyk
Springfield-Hanby Lodge No. 767
Springfield, Pennsylvania
September 12, 2009

---

1. Lomas, Robert. The Secret Science of Masonic Initiation. Hersham, Surrey, UK: Lewis Masonic. 2008

Sunday
The Compasses

The craftsman stretches out his rule,
He marks one out with chalk;
He fashions it with a plane,
He marks it out with a compass,
And makes it like the figure of a man,
According to the beauty of a man,
That it may remain in the house.

Isaiah 44:12-14

Circumscribe thy desires this day,
keeping them within due bounds toward all.

Sunday Morning
The Sun rises in the East,
to Open and Rule the Day

Great Architect of the Universe, as the Sun rises in the East to open and rule the day, so may I govern my thoughts this day with Justice and Equity toward all. May I be inspired by the Mason's Compasses to circumscribe my desires and keep them within due bounds toward all people, especially my Brethren in Freemasonry. May I measure with accuracy the state of my soul, that I may be true to myself this day, and walk together in concert and harmony with my fellow man. *So Mote It Be.*

Strictly speaking, the Compasses are not mentioned as a Working Tool in any of the Degrees. This means that the Compasses belong to all Freemasons. As they are the principal Tool of initial drafting for the Architect, so they are the principal Tool of initial preparation for the Mason's spiritual journey. It is well known that the Compasses teach us to circumscribe our desires. This limiting of the extent of self-interest is a good place to begin. But further, as the Compasses may be used to measure the span of a stone, or the width of a mortar joint, so ought we each day to measure the span of our good will toward all mankind, the breadth of our knowledge, and the width of our mercy. Only by so measuring will we come to know ourselves, and only then can we, in the words of Shakespeare's Polonius, to our own selves be true.

Sunday Morning

This Morning may I
* Take the measure of my own sense of Justice and Equity
* Seek out another in need of personal Justice and help him find it
* Set to rights one incident of inequity that I may come upon
* Agree to walk with another whom I may find difficult, in something important to him
* Spend a few moments meditating upon the meaning of the Compasses in these actions

Great Architect of the Universe, I pray this Morning for all my Brethren in Freemasonry, and for all my fellow human beings, who suffer from:
* Injustice because of race, religion, nationality, gender, personal beliefs, place in society, or any other reason, especially (Names . . .)
* Or from an insufficient measure on my own part of mercy, empathy, understanding, or care, especially (Names . . .)
May you look out for them this Morning, and may I have the opportunity, if possible, to set things right.
So Mote It Be.

Sunday Noon
The Sun at High Meridian,
the Beauty and Glory of the Day

Great Architect of the Universe, as the blazing Sun at High Meridian shows forth the beauty and glory of the day, so may I be refreshed by the beauty I find in the world around me and, amidst the round of my daily labors, may I take the time to glory in the presence of my fellow man as we walk together in unity of spirit and purpose.
So Mote It Be.

The perfect circle, found nowhere in Nature save when inscribed by the arms of the Compasses working together in harmony, bears witness to the beauty of human cooperation. Just as Freemasons are united as a Band of Brothers among whom no contention should ever exist, so the Compasses teach us to seek union and peace with all creatures. As the circle of the Sun at High Meridian bathes the earth in light, so are we bathed in the light of understanding and knowledge when we use the Compasses to take the measure of our own lives. The circle inscribed by the Compasses need not be restrictive, but may be *inclusive*, including within the circle of our own lives others who may have been, or have felt to be, on the outside.

Sunday Noon

This Afternoon May I:
* Find a person whom I had drawn out of the circle of my life, and
* Draw my circle a little wider, to include that person within it
* Take a few moments to measure my own sense of beauty in the world
* Try to see the beauty in another that no one else sees
* Spend a few moments meditating upon the meaning of the Compasses in these actions

Great Architect of the Universe, I pray this Afternoon for all my Brethren in Freemasonry, and for all my fellow human beings, who suffer from:
* Circles that are too small, either of their own or others' making, especially (Names . . .)
* Or from aspects of their own lives, personalities, or physical appearances that others may not find beautiful, especially (Names . . .)
May you look out for them this Afternoon, and may I have the opportunity, if possible, to set things right.
So Mote It Be.

Sunday Evening
The Sun sets in the West,
to Close the Day

Great Architect of the Universe, as the Sun sets in the West to close the day, so may I prepare to bring my day to a close with honor and grace. Help me to be satisfied with what you have given me this day, and to freely offer to all men what is their due from me. Teach me the wages of self-understanding and truth, and grant me, now at the end of the day, the inestimable gift of a satisfied heart.
So Mote It Be.

How often do proclaim, "I only ask what is coming to me"? As if we could be certain that we have earned all those things we dearly desire to possess! But all too often what is "coming to us," what we consider our due, is so much less or at least so much other than what we believe we deserve. What if our insight were as sharp as the Compasses, so that we might accurately measure the recompense we truly deserve for the work we have actually done during the day past? What if we were willing to extend the Compasses' points to span the difference between what we truly owe others and what we have been willing to give? What if our goal at the end of every day were to see that none might leave our presence dissatisfied?

Sunday Evening

This Evening may I:
* Speak with someone near to me and be sure I have given them their due attention this day
* Extend the points of my heart's Compasses to measure the span between what I ought to have given and what I actually gave, and
* Meditate upon whether I am satisfied with what I have found
* As I prepare for bed, give thanks to God for my daily bread
* Spend a few moments meditating upon the meaning of the Compasses in these actions

Great Architect of the Universe, I pray this Evening for all my Brethren in Freemasonry, and for all my fellow human beings, who suffer from:
* Dashed hopes and unfulfilled dreams, especially (Names . . .)
* Or from ways in which I may have disappointed them, known or unknown to me, especially (Names . . .)
May you look out for them this Night, and may I have the opportunity, if possible, to set things right.
So Mote It Be.

Monday
The Twenty-four Inch Gauge

But I, by your great mercy,
     will come into your house;
     in reverence will I bow down
     toward your holy temple.
Lead me, O LORD, in your righteousness
     because of my enemies,
     make straight your way before me.
          Psalms 5:7-9

Make thy paths straight this day,
and plan thy life in good measure.

Monday Morning
The Sun rises in the East,
to Open and Rule the Day

Great Architect of the Universe, as the Sun rises in the East to open and rule the day, so may I govern my thoughts and deeds this day with Justice and Equity toward all. May I be inspired by the Twenty-four Inch Gauge to measure my time, that it may be divided well between my services to God and my Brethren, my daily vocations, and my needed rest and refreshment. *So Mote It Be*.

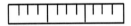

The Twenty-four Inch Gauge is a reminder of the cubit, by which length was the Temple of Solomon measured and laid out. We divide it into three equal parts to teach us that the twenty-four hours of the day are to be divided into three equally balanced segments that include rest, work, and service. Even so was the Temple's *Sanctum Sanctorum*, the Holy of Holies, of equal measure on each side. This perfect cube housed the Ark of the Covenant, the place where God, at that time, dwelled with His people. We have, therefore, no less an example than the House of God to show us the importance of a three-fold balance in the ordering of our day. It is equally important to serve God, our Brother, and our fellow man, to diligently perform the work of our occupation, and to allow ourselves the rest and refreshment we need to perform those duties. In all these ways do we provide for our families and ourselves.

Monday Morning

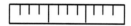

This Morning may I:
* Plan the tasks of my day in equal measure
* Spend time in prayer, and service to God
* Learn about a Masonic Charity, or a charity in my home town
* Seek to begin my day rested and relaxed
* Spend a few moments meditating upon the meaning of the Twenty-four Inch Gauge in these actions

Great Architect of the Universe, I pray this Morning for all my Brethren in Freemasonry, and all my fellow human beings, who suffer from:
* An inability to plan balance in their lives because of illness, economic distress, or vocational demands, especially (Names . . .)
* Or from inordinate demands I may make upon them, or myself, that deprive them, or me, of such balance, especially (Names . . .)
May you look out for them this Morning, and may I have the opportunity, if possible, to set things right.
So Mote It Be.

Monday Noon
The Sun at High Meridian,
the Beauty and Glory of the Day

Great Architect of the Universe, as the blazing Sun at High Meridian shows forth the beauty and glory of the day, so may I be refreshed by the beauty I find in the world around me and, amidst the round of my daily labors, may I seek to lend my talents and abilities in vast profusion to those who may benefit thereby, seeking always to lend a helping hand wherever I may. *So Mote It Be*.

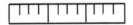

A balanced stewardship of time is not the only lesson of the Twenty-four Inch Gauge, even though it is the twenty-four hours in the day to which its divisions refer. We are also admonished to be good stewards of our talents, abilities, and gifts for work and service. A Freemason seeks to be helpful wherever and in as many ways as he can. A balanced use of our talent not only increases the number of those who may benefit from our skills, but it also helps to develop us into a more well-rounded person. We may be well aware of the talents which suit our chosen vocation. But we may not have dwelt upon what talents and abilities we have to offer our Lodge, our place of worship, or the many organizations in our community. Are the talents we possess being put to their best uses? What talents might we have that could better enable us to find refreshment, and experience the beauty of the world around us?

Monday Noon

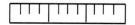

This Afternoon May I:
* Take inventory of the talents and abilities I am using this day
* Use a new talent, or use an old talent in a new way, just for fun
* Ask at least one person, "What can I do for you?"
* Think of at least one way to build upon the talents that I have
* Spend a few moments meditating upon the meaning of the Twenty-four Inch Gauge in these actions

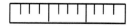

Great Architect of the Universe, I pray this Afternoon for all my Brethren in Freemasonry, and all my fellow human beings, who suffer from:
* An inability to develop their natural talents because they are poor, or ill, or not accepted in society, especially (Names . . .)
* Or from a talent or ability that I might be using to assist them, but have not done so, especially, (Names . . .)
May you look out for them this Afternoon, and may I have the opportunity, if possible, to set things right.
So Mote It Be.

Monday Evening
The Sun sets in the West,
to Close the Day

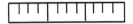

Great Architect of the Universe, as the Sun sets in the West to close the day, so may I prepare to bring my day to a close with honor and grace. Help me to see the beauty of the world at dusk, and of the starry heavens. As I look back over the day past, show me how I might have better distributed my treasure among my fellow men, and help me to measure my generosity by the straightedge of your loving will. *So Mote It Be*.

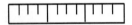

The final aspect of our lives over which we are called to exercise a balanced stewardship is the one we tend to find most problematical: that of our treasure; more especially the *money* that God has entrusted to our safekeeping. There are so many demands made upon the money we take in and store up that we are tempted to fear there will never be enough, even for our basic needs. Indeed there are those, even among our Brethren in the Craft, who may not have enough to get by, let alone to give to others. But most of us have something to spare; perhaps only a little, perhaps a vast sum. We have promised to help, aid and assist all poor and penniless Brother Master Masons applying to us for aid as such. And we know this promise also applies to all our fellow men. But do we actually seek them out to offer help, or do we remain quiet, hoping they may not find us? Are we straight with ourselves about that question?

Monday Evening

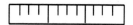

This Evening may I:
*   Study my checkbook or bank account, and see what I might be able to give away to someone in need this week
*   Go outside and look at the beauty of the starry heavens, and
*   Meditate upon God's great abundance, in Nature and in my life
*   As I prepare for bed, give thanks to God for the many blessings he has seen fit to bestow upon me
*   Spend a few moments meditating upon the meaning of the Twenty-four Inch Gauge, or the Straightedge, in these actions

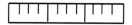

Great Architect of the Universe, I pray this Evening for all my Brethren in Freemasonry, and all my fellow human beings, who suffer from:
*   A lack of enough money to get by, especially
    (Names . . .)
*   Or from my own failure to give generously when I might have done so, especially (Names . . .)
May you look out for them this Night, and may I have the opportunity, if possible, to set things right.
So Mote It Be.

Tuesday
The Common Gavel

The prophet that hath a dream, let him
tell a dream; and he that hath my word,
let him speak my word faithfully. What
is the chaff to the wheat? saith the LORD.
Is not my word like as a fire? saith the
LORD; and like a hammer that breaketh
the rock in pieces?

Break off thy rough corners this day,
and make thyself as a fit stone.

Tuesday Morning
The Sun rises in the East,
to Open and Rule the Day

Great Architect of the Universe, as the Sun rises in the East to open and rule the day, so may I govern my thoughts and deeds this day that I may trim from them the rough corners of selfishness and injustice which I show toward the world. May I be inspired by the Common Gavel to trim and shape the rough ashlar at the core of my being, making me a smoother stone better fit for that house not made with hands. *So Mote It Be.*

The Masonic Common Gavel is not the implement used by judges, or auctioneers.   Rather, it is the traditional stonemason's hammer, an implement whose iron head is flat at one end like a hammer, and tapered at the other end in a chisel-like shape. This *gabled*, or *gaveled*, end gives it the name. It is a hammer and a chisel in one implement. In dressing stones, the chisel end is used to incise a cut-line, the hammer end then being used to knock off the unwanted side of the cut. The chisel end is also used for the more delicate removal of small defects when the full blow of a hammer would be too much.   As we seek personal conversion by divesting our hearts and consciences of the vices and superfluities of life, it is important to know when a careful, surgical chipping is needed, or when the dramatic impact of a hammer blow.

Tuesday Morning

The Morning may I:
* Chip some annoying little vice from the rough ashlar of my life
* Make a list of the trivial superfluities that make me less than what I might be, and begin to hammer away upon at least one of them
* Take aim with the Gavel of my intent at one inequity I see in my world
* Spend a few moments meditating upon the meaning of the Common Gavel in these actions

Great Architect of the Universe, I pray this Morning for all my Brethren in Freemasonry, and for all my fellow human beings, who suffer from:
* My being a rough instead of a smooth ashlar, especially (Names . . .)
* Or from the wild and unskillful swinging of a heavy hammer upon them by others for their faults or shortcomings, especially (Names . . .)
May you look out for them this Morning, and may I have the opportunity, if possible, to set things right.
So Mote It Be.

Tuesday Noon
The Sun at High Meridian,
the Beauty and Glory of the Day

Great Architect of the Universe, as the blazing Sun at High Meridian shows forth the beauty and glory of the day, so may I learn to use my Working Tools for beauty as well as utility. Help me to chip away all that is less than beautiful in my spirit, that I may become the glorious work of art you plan for me to be, and grant that I might cause and allow others to do so as well. *So Mote It Be.*

There is more than strength and utility in a block of stone. There is beauty hidden within, as well. A great block of marble may become part of the wall of a temple, losing its own identity as it fades into the many rows and tiers of other stones. But that same block of marble may have hidden away within it a Michelangelo's *David*, or a *Venus de Milo*. So it is with our own lives. There is more than usefulness hidden away within a human being. We are none of us created simply to be used. There is beauty also. Sometimes it is readily apparent, sometimes it may only be seen by a sculptor the likes of the Great Architect, Himself. When we learn to wield the stonemason's hammer, how to measure and balance the delicate tap and the mighty blow, we begin to learn how to look into the unworked stone of our own lives and envision the beauty that lies within. And then, amazingly, we begin also to see the beauty in others.

Tuesday Noon

This Afternoon may I:
* Look for beauty within one other person
* Make a list of what is beautiful in myself
* Keep chipping away at that annoying little vice
* Buy a little statue to put on my desk or bookshelf
* Spend a few moments meditating upon the meaning of the Common Gavel in these actions

Great Architect of the Universe, I pray this Afternoon for all my Brethren in Freemasonry, and all my fellow human beings, who suffer from:
* An inability to see the beauty within their own lives, especially (Names . . .)
* Or from an errant blow inflicted by my own hammer, especially (Names . . .)
May you look out for them this Afternoon, and my I have the opportunity, if possible, to set things right.
So Mote It Be.

Tuesday Evening
The Sun sets in the West,
to Close the Day

Great Architect of the Universe, as the Sun sets in the West to close the day, so may I prepare to bring my day to a close with honor and grace. May I wipe from my stonemason's hammer the dust of the day past, polish out the scratches made by the hard granite of my own stubbornness, and carefully put it away that it might rest in the quiet darkness of night, to ring out upon stone again in the morning. *So Mote It Be.*

The end of the day was the traditional time for payment of the day's wages, as the worksite was closed and workmen lined up at the gate to receive their pay before going home to their families and their rest. The Common Gavel, the stonemason's hammer, is not an easy tool to wield. We finish the day with muscles aching, clothes dirty, skin covered in dust. But we have done our job, and our wages are due. There may be inequities in the world, and unfair labor practices, but not within the employ of the Great Architect of the Universe. When we realize for whom we labor, and the work we are called to do, we can never go away dissatisfied at the day's end. No, we shall never go away dissatisfied at the end of the day, nor ought we ever be the cause of such dissatisfaction in another.

Tuesday Evening

This Evening may I:
* Reflect upon the ways in which I may have experienced conversion in my life this day; how have I become a different person?
* Make a list of the things in my life that still need smoothing out
* Learn to use a hammer without hitting my thumb
* Imagine when I may finally finish chipping away at that annoying little vice
* Spend a few moments meditating upon the meaning of the Common Gavel in these actions

Great Architect of the Universe, I pray this Evening for all my Brethren in Freemasonry, and all my fellow human beings, who suffer from:
* Lack of conversion in some important part of their lives, especially (Names . . .)
* Or from being injured in body or spirit by the rough corners of unfinished persons around them, especially (Names . . .)
May you look out for them this Night, and may I have the opportunity, if possible, to set things right. *So Mote It Be.*

Wednesday
The Plumb

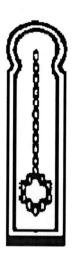

This is what he showed me: the LORD was
standing by a wall that had been built to true
plumb, with a plumb line in His hand. And
the LORD asked me, "What do you see, Amos?"
"A plumb line," I replied. Then the LORD said,
"Look, I am setting a plumb line among my
people Israel . . . " Amos 7:7-9

See that thou may walk uprightly this day,
before God and man.

Wednesday Morning
The Sun rises in the East,
to Open and Rule the Day

Great Architect of the Universe, as the Sun rises in the East to open and rule the day, so may I govern my thoughts and deeds this day, that when you set your Plumb line beside my soul you will not find me wanting as a champion of Justice and Equity for all people. May I walk uprightly all the day long in my vocation, my avocations, and my family life, and may I not falter in my obligations before God and man. *So Mote It Be.*

We have begun the week in personal introspection and conversion. Now with the Plumb we come to the Fellowcraft Working Tools, and our growth together in community with our Brethren in Freemasonry. Operative stonemasons use the Plumb to insure a true vertical in a stone wall, so as it rises tier upon tier, the force of gravity will remain contained within the wall's outer dimensions, and it will not slip or topple over. As Free and Accepted Masons we learn from the Plumb to stand uprightly, as a well-built wall, in our several walks of life before God and man. This personal integrity is more than just self-improvement. It is the core of all human community. For only when we act with integrity can we be depended upon to be a part of any community. And any community, as any temple, is only as strong as its weakest wall.

Wednesday Morning

This Morning may I:
* Vow to treat everyone I meet with uprightness of heart, and rectitude of conduct
* Read from the Book of Amos, or one of the other Prophets, and apply God's Plumb line to my life
* Ask, What part of my life is farthest out of Plumb? What will I do about it?
* Spend a few moments meditating upon the meaning of the Plumb in these actions

Great Architect of the Universe, I pray this Morning for all my Brethren in Freemasonry, and for all my fellow human beings, who suffer from:
* Having been cheated by a friend, a business contact, a family member, or a Brother, especially (Names . . .)
* Or for some out-of-Plumb part of my own life, especially, (Names . . .)
May you look out for them this Morning, and may I have the opportunity, if possible, to set things right.
So Mote It Be.

Wednesday Noon
The Sun at High Meridian,
the Beauty and Glory of the Day

Great Architect of the Universe, as the blazing sun at High Meridian shows forth the beauty and glory of the day, so may your true Plumb line produce in me the beauty and glory of an upright symmetry of words and deeds, that I may stand erect and not fall, as I seek to know and do your will among my fellow men. *So Mote It Be.*

There is something remarkable about the human eye and inner ear that combine in the mind to ascribe beauty to the upright structure. A leaning tower may be an intriguing curiosity, but it is not beautiful. Just as we find visual beauty in bilateral symmetry, so we find beauty in vertical symmetry. When a man walks uprightly through the day in his several stations in life, he is not merely dependable; in his spirit he is beautiful, and partakes in the heavenly glory of the Great Architect of the Universe. Whether in labor or refreshment, uprightness of heart and rectitude of conduct are the goals of a Freemason. When all its stones fit together, one upon one in true vertical alignment, a wall is said to have integrity. When we have fit our thoughts, words, and deeds one upon one in true alignment, we have integrity as well, and measure up to the divine Plumb line.

Wednesday Noon

This Afternoon may I:
* Construct a Plumb line with a string and a stone, hold it in front of me at arm's length, and walk slowly forward, then meditate on what it means to stray neither to the right nor the left
* Think of someone I know who I would describe as upright, and write down his or her qualities as I see them
* Do the right thing, even when I don't want to
* Spend a few moments meditating on the meaning of the Plumb in these actions

Great Architect of the Universe, I pray this Afternoon for all my Brethren in Freemasonry, and all my fellow human beings, who suffer from:
* Old, broken, or twisted bodies, preventing them from walking physically upright, especially (Names . . .)
* Or from my failure to do the right thing, even when I knew better, especially (Names . . .)
May you look out for them this Afternoon, and may I have the opportunity, if possible, to set things right.
So Mote It Be.

Wednesday Evening
The Sun sets in the West,
to Close the Day

Great Architect of the Universe, as the Sun sets in the West to close the day, so may I prepare to bring my day to a close with honor and grace. May the uprightness of my heart and the rectitude of my conduct have been a blessing to someone today, an inspiration to another, a sign of hope to all. May I not be satisfied until your Plumb line finds me straight and true in all my works. *So Mote It Be*.

In addition to proving true verticals, the Plumb line has another purpose, equally as important, if less well known. It provides a way of lining up two points one over the other, that must be in a straight vertical line. For example, marks to drill holes in a wall in which to place anchor bolts for the hanging of a vertical beam or a cabinet. Once the first hole is marked, a Plumb line dropped from or through it will give the line upon which the second hole is to be marked. In our moral lives, the Great Architect of the Universe holds the beginning of the Plumb line, and lets it hang down. If we are to be "in line" with Him, it will be along that line we will find our own mark.

Wednesday Evening

This Evening may I:
* Draw a Plumb line on a piece of paper. Label the point at the top "Great Architect." Halfway down the line, mark a point representing "Me," as far to the left or the right of "plumb" as I feel myself to be. Put the paper in my wallet, to look at and revise each Wednesday evening, until I am satisfied
* Think of a recent time when I have been less than honest. Decide what to do about it
* Spend a few moments meditating upon the meaning of the Plumb in these actions

Great Architect of the Universe, I pray this Evening for all my Brethren in Freemasonry, and for all my fellow human beings, who suffer from:
* Having no wages, or who find their lives unsatisfying, especially (Names . . .)
* Or from being unjustly judged by someone else's idea of what is "plumb," especially (Names . . .)
May you look out for them this Night, and may I have the opportunity, if possible, to set things right. *So Mote It Be.*

Thursday
The Level

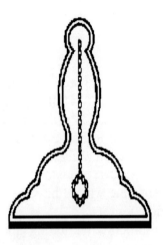

" . . . and I will make justice the plumb line,
and righteousness the level; then hail will
sweep away the refuge of lies, and the
waters will overflow the secret place."
Isaiah 28:17

Travel upon the level of time this day,
with justice and righteousness.

Thursday Morning
The Sun rises in the East,
to Open and Rule the Day

Great Architect of the Universe, as the Sun rises in the East to open and rule the day, so may I govern my thoughts and deeds this day, that I may walk upon that level highway whereon all men are fellow travelers on our way to that Undiscovered Country. Help me to remember that time and tide favor no man but indeed treat us all alike, and strengthen me this day to do the same for all I meet.
So Mote It Be.

Equality is the meaning of the second Fellowcraft Working Tool. One might expect equality to be measured on the scales, or by a ruler. But the Level gives us a far more profound picture of what equality really is. In the journey through time, from birth to the grave, each of us travels upon the same level path. True, there are ups and downs, mountains and valleys. And they are different for every man. They are the experiences of life. But time moves the same for all, whether through bad times or good, and upon the road of time we are all treading upon the same level, we are all equal travelers. This is an important thing to remember when we are tempted to see others as "below" or "above" us. Once we have learned the lesson the Level, and see all men as truly equal, we are in sight of the goal of Brotherly Love, the mark of a Master Mason.

Thursday Morning

This Morning may I:
* See everyone I meet as a fellow-traveler on the way to the grave
* Carry someone else's burden for a little while along that path
* Treat everyone with whom I deal "on the level," that is, equally
* Learn something about a civil rights movement I have neglected
* Spend a few moments meditating upon the meaning of the Level in these actions

Great Architect of the Universe, I pray this Morning for all my Brethren in Freemasonry, and for all my fellow human beings, who suffer from:
* Inequality of treatment or esteem on my part, especially (Names . . .)
* Or from practicing their own version of bigotry or discrimination, especially (Names . . .)
May you look out for them this Morning, and may I have the opportunity, if possible, to set things right.
So Mote It Be.

Thursday Noon
The Sun at High Meridian,
the Beauty and Glory of the Day

Great Architect of the Universe, as the blazing Sun at High Meridian shows forth the beauty and glory of the day, so may the level plane of a good heart be the basis for beauty in my relations with my fellow man, that we may travel together in that universal peace and tranquility which pervades the community of men who honor and respect one another. *So Mote It Be.*

"Is that on the Level?" is a question we have all heard or asked at some point, and it usually has the connotation of "are you being honest with me?" or "are you treating me fairly?" But that meaning comes from an even deeper question, "Are you treating me as an equal, with equal consideration to that with which you treat yourself?" Expressed this way, one can see the Level is indeed a symbol of that universal axiom of all religions, of all spiritualities: The Golden Rule. "In everything, do to others as you would have them do to you; for this is [the meaning of] the law and the prophets." (*Matthew 7:11*) "And what you hate, do not do to anyone." (*Tobit 4:15*) "None of you [truly] believes until he wishes for his brother that which he wishes for himself." (*13 of Imam Al-Nawai's "Forty Hadiths."*) In other words, so far as it is possible for us, we ought always to grant everyone a level playing field in life.

Thursday Noon

This Afternoon may I:
* Visit a cemetery, and walk among the graves
* Read *all* the obituaries in my local newspaper
* Figure out the approximate number of seconds that have elapsed in my life so far
* Give someone an equal shot at something I am striving for
* Spend a few moments meditating upon the meaning of the Level in these actions

Great Architect of the Universe, I pray this Afternoon for all my Brethren in Freemasonry, and for all my fellow human beings, who suffer from:
* Having to climb a steeper hill than I, or from sliding down a more slippery slope, especially (Names . . .)
* Or from being hindered by obstacles I have put in their way, especially (Names . . .)
May you look out for them this Afternoon, and may I have the opportunity, if possible, to set things right.
So Mote It Be.

Thursday Evening
The Sun sets in the West,
to Close the Day

Great Architect of the Universe, as the Sun sets in the West to close the day, so may I prepare to bring my day to a close with honor and grace. May I entrust equally everyone I know to my thoughts and prayers this night, and in the morning may I treat equally everyone I meet, helping to lower mountains and raise valleys, that my fellow men may have a level pathway for their feet. *So Mote It Be.*

Have you ever tried to "eyeball" hanging a picture on the wall? Or worse yet a set of kitchen cabinets, or a chair rail? The human eye is a marvelous thing, but it is not perfect. Eyesight varies from person to person, or in one person from morning to evening. Some of us can see the "level," others cannot hang something straight for the life of us. The same is true with moral judgment. Our human abilities in that field are just not perfect. Sometimes we can see the level solution, often we cannot. As a Working Tool, the stonemason's Level teaches us that we need an objective, outside guide to help us discern what is truly level. In this matter, the Greatest of all Architects is the greatest Guide, and the Volume of Sacred Law is a most excellent Tool.

Thursday Evening

This Evening may I:
* Make at least some part of someone's life easier for them
* When I pay, or repay, someone for a kindness done for me, be sure their wages are just
* Try drawing freehand a straight, level line on a wall or blackboard, then check it with a Straightedge and a Level
* Spend a few moments meditating upon the meaning of the Level in these actions

Great Architect of the Universe, I pray this Evening for all my Brethren in Freemasonry, and all my fellow human beings, who suffer from:
* Having to prove themselves over and over again in the face of prejudice, especially (Names . . .)
* Or are nearing their journey's end on the "level of time," especially (Names . . .)
May you look out for them this Night, and may I have the opportunity, if possible, to set things right. *So Mote It Be*.

Friday
The Square

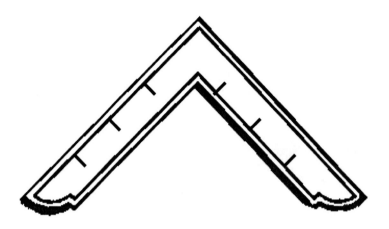

And the altar shall be twelve cubits long, twelve broad, square in the four squares thereof.　　　Ezekiel 43:16-18

Square thine actions this day, with the square of virtue.

Friday Morning
The Sun rises in the East,
to Open and Rule the Day

Great Architect of the Universe, as the Sun rises in the East to open and rule the day, so may I govern my thoughts and deeds this day, that in all my doings I may square my actions by the Square of virtue, and in all my relationships be fair to all I meet. May I have so learned from the Plumb, and the Level, that all the angles in my life may meet on the Square. *So Mote It Be*.

Men have been making lists of virtues from out of the mists of time. Indeed, we seem more capable of listing virtues than of living them. In his *Republic*, Plato listed four virtues: Wisdom, Courage, Moderation, and Justice. Theologians such as Augustine of Hippo and Thomas Aquinas listed Prudence, Justice, Restraint, and Courage. From Paul of Tarsus in the New Testament come Faith, Hope, and Love. A survey of various lists of knightly virtues from the Middle Ages gives us Courage, Justice, Mercy, Generosity, Faith, Nobility, and Hope. Benjamin Franklin had a list of thirteen virtues, that included Silence, Humility, and Moderation. When we set out to square our actions by the Square of virtue, we mean all these things. Yet we also mean something far simpler and yet far more profound: We will treat others fairly. "Fairly" does not mean what they have earned, but according to what they are: fellow human beings.

Friday Morning

This Morning may I:
* Make my own list of virtues, and add to or revise this list each Friday
* Choose just one virtue to work on this Morning
* Be silent once, instead of shouting out; voice the truth instead of remaining silent
* Learn something new about the word "mercy"
* Spend a few moments meditating upon the meaning of the Square in these actions

Great Architect of the Universe, I pray this Morning for all my Brethren in Freemasonry, and for all my fellow human beings, who suffer from:
* Unfair treatment in the workplace or in the market, especially (Names . . .)
* Or from a lack of Faith, or Hope, or Love, especially (Names . . .)
May you look out for them this Morning, and may I have the opportunity, if possible, to set things right.
So Mote It Be.

Friday Noon
The Sun at High Meridian,
the Beauty and Glory of the Day

Great Architect of the Universe, as the blazing sun at High Meridian shows forth the beauty and glory of the day, so may the practice of many virtues cultivate beauty in my life, and in the world. May I experience this day the moral refreshment that comes from intentional virtue, and may I approach my fellow man squarely, in fairness of thought and deed. *So Mote It Be*.

Quadrilateral figures come in all shapes and sizes. But if all four lines are of equal length, then all four angles will also be equal. They will be right angles, and the figure we will have will be a square. The third Working Tool of the Fellowcraft Mason (representing one angle and two sides of a square) builds upon the lessons of the Plumb and the Level. For a man of personal integrity who understands the inherent equality of all men will treat them all fairly. Fairness is the chief lesson of the Square, and is itself an important virtue. When we ask, "Is it a square deal?" we mean, "Is it fair to all involved?" All participants in a square deal experience equal boundaries, equal opportunities, equal standing. Perhaps the core idea of the "Public Square" is a place where all people deal fairly with each other in their various transactions of business, politics, friendship, or sport.

Friday Noon

This Afternoon may I:
* Keep working on that virtue I chose this Morning
* Learn the difference between Knowledge and Wisdom
* Make a list of terms that begin or end with "-square-" and add to that list whenever I think of a new one. What do I learn from this?
* Spend some time in a Public Square, really looking at the people
*Spend a few moments meditating upon the meaning of the Square in these actions

Great Architect of the Universe, I pray this Afternoon for all my Brethren in Freemasonry, and for all my fellow human beings, who suffer from:
* Never being offered, or never offering, a square deal in life, especially (Names . . .)
* Or from being held to someone else's false idea of virtue, especially (Names . . .)
May you look out for them this Afternoon, and may I have the opportunity, if possible, to set things right.
So Mote It Be.

Friday Evening
The Sun sets in the West,
to Close the Day

Great Architect of the Universe, as the Sun sets in the West to close the day, so may I prepare to bring my day to a close with honor and grace. May I come to the ending of each day knowing that I have treated everyone fairly, "on the square," and that I have grown in the practice of virtue. So shall I have paid my debt to you and to mankind, and so shall I be satisfied. *So Mote It Be.*

In today's vernacular, when we call someone "a square" we mean he is dull and old-fashioned, and we are intending not to pay him a compliment. But we misunderstand the implications of the words we use. In a world where sharp words injure, and sharp swords kill, there is perhaps some room for the quiet peace of dullness. And something made the old way (the meaning of old-fashioned) may be sturdier or more reliable than its cheaper, mass-produced modern replacement. Old-fashioned does not need to mean "out-of-date." It may mean "solid, and having endured the test of time." Like Freemasonry, the virtues have endured the moral test of ages. They work. They are old friends. There is nothing wrong with being "square," if by that we mean to be steeped in the ancient virtues. It's only fair.

Friday Evening

This Evening may I:
* Keep working on that virtue I chose this Morning
* Learn the relationship between Justice and Mercy
* Look myself "squarely in the eye." What do I see?
* Spend a few moments meditating upon the meaning of the Square in these actions

Great Architect of the Universe, I pray this Evening for all my Brethren in Freemasonry, and all my fellow human beings, who suffer from:
* Being considered old-fashioned, or out-of-date, or irrelevant, or unnecessary, or just plain old, especially (Names . . .)
* Or not being welcome in the Public Square, especially (Names . . .)
May you look out for them this Night, and may I have the opportunity, if possible, to set things right. *So Mote It Be.*

Saturday
The Trowel

When you have crossed the Jordan into
the land the LORD your God is giving you,
set up some large stones and coat them
with plaster. Write on them the words of
this Law . . .   Deuteronomy 27:1-3

Spread this day in abundance
the mortar of Brotherly Love

Saturday Morning
The Sun rises in the East,
to Open and Rule the Day

Great Architect of the Universe, as the Sun rises in the East to open and rule the day, so may I govern my thoughts and deeds this day that I may wield within my beloved Craft the Trowel of a Master Mason to spread the cement of brotherly love and affection through all my thoughts, words, and deeds, treating all I meet with Justice and Equity. *So Mote It Be.*

Alone among the Working Tools, and thus dramatically ironic for the primary tool of a Master Mason, the Trowel is not an implement of the architect. It is a tool of laboring amid the sweat and strain of the building site. It is the final step, after the design has been drawn, the stones cut, measured and squared, when the temple is at last put together. So it is that the final responsibility is with the workman upon the wall. His job it is to "set in stone" for ages to come the combined work of the other tools. This teaches us that "Brotherly Love" is no abstract or esoteric concept. It is sublimely practical, and as immediate to human experience as labor and grit, sweat and strain. The moment of truth comes when the Mason dips his Trowel into the bucket, ladles out and smoothly spreads the mortar, and sets the next stone into place. So it is with Brotherly Love and Affection: the moment of truth comes when we go beyond the theory and promise, and reach a hand out to our Brother.

Saturday Morning

This Morning may I:
* Call at least one man I meet "Brother," whether he is of the Craft or not
* Look at a mortared wall, and imagine the Mason who built it
* Show someone genuine love and affection in a practical way.
* Imagine my life as a mortared wall. Where is the mortar in need of repair?
* Spend a few moments meditating upon the meaning of the Trowel in these actions

Great Architect of the Universe, I pray this Morning for all my Brethren in Freemasonry, and for all my fellow human beings, who suffer from:
* Having no one near to call "My Brother," especially (Names . . .)
* Or from a lack of love and affection that I might have offered, especially (Names . . .)
May you look out for them this Morning, and may I have the opportunity, if possible, to set things right.
So Mote It Be.

Saturday Noon
The Sun at High Meridian,
the Beauty and Glory of the Day

Great Architect of the Universe, as the blazing Sun at High Meridian shows forth the beauty and glory of the day, so might I, like spreading spotless white plaster upon a finished work, show forth the beauty of Brotherly Love in my world. May this Brotherhood be the crowning glory of all my works this day, so that others may look upon it and know the love which Masons bear toward one another.
So Mote It Be.

As the children of Israel prepared to cross the Jordan River into the Land of Promise, Moses delivered to them a final command, to set up an altar of stones upon Mount Ebal in the central highlands, and to cover the stones with plaster to provide a smooth surface for writing. Upon the plaster, after it had been smoothed with the Trowels of Masons, they were to write the words of the Volume of Sacred Law handed down to them in the wilderness, as a witness to their devotion and commitment. (Deuteronomy 27:1-8) High upon the shoulder of the mountain, this white plastered altar would catch the Sun and shine out for many miles, the beauty and glory of a covenant with God. So the Mason's trowel is not an implement of construction only, but a tool of art whereby the glory of faith may be made manifest, and the beauty of brotherhood witnessed to.

Saturday Noon

This Afternoon may I:
* Pick up a rough stone, hold it in my hands, and envision it smoothed and polished, gleaming with white plaster
* Treat yet another person with genuine love and affection in a practical way
* Show true sympathy to someone in despair, be of service to someone who needs help, or make a real sacrifice on behalf of another
* Spend a few moments meditating upon the meaning of the Trowel in these actions

Great Architect of the Universe, I pray this Afternoon for all my Brethren in Freemasonry, and all my fellow human beings, who suffer from:
* Loneliness, alienation, or loss, especially (Names . . .)
* Or from my own lack of showing brotherly love and affection, especially (Names . . .)
May you look out for them this Afternoon, and may I have the opportunity, if possible, to set things right.
So Mote It Be.

Saturday Evening

The Sun sets in the West,
to Close the Day

Great Architect of the Universe, as the Sun sets in the West to close the day, so may I prepare to bring my day to a close with honor and grace. May I have this day paid all my family, friends, and Brothers their due wages of Brotherly Love and Affection, that none may have gone away from me dissatisfied. As I begin upon the morrow a new week, may the Working Tools of Freemasonry be to me a guide to my actions, and a beacon to my hope.
So Mote It Be.

The Working Tools of Freemasonry have been called "the evangelists of a new day." They are teachers not less than the college and the cathedral. Just as the Twenty-four Inch Gauge and Common Gavel stand for stewardship and conversion; the Plumb, Level, and Square present basic ideas of integrity, equality and fairness; so the Trowel is Freemasonry's symbol of Brotherly Love and Affection, which is the binding together and culmination of the work of all the other tools. (Adapted and modified from the Masonic Short Talk Bulletin, vol. 6 no. 4, April 1928) In this tool of the Master Mason are combined the sublimely symbolic and the purely practical, which is as it should be, for Freemasonry proclaims "As above, so below;" the unity of the heavenly and earthly realms, of spirit and flesh, of mind and matter.

Saturday Evening

This Evening may I:
* Make a list of those with whom I will try to cement a better fellowship in the coming week
* Look back at the list I made last week to see how I have done
* Spend time especially with my family, or with a friend
* Spend a few moments meditating upon the meaning of the Trowel in these actions

Great Architect of the Universe, I pray this Evening for all my Brethren in Freemasonry, and all my fellow human beings, who are:
* Celebrating the joyous events of life's milestones: Birthdays, Births, Weddings, Anniversaries, or Good News, especially (Names . . .)
* Dealing with life's sorrows: Illness, Death, Separation, or Loss, especially (Names . . .)
May you look out for them this Night, and may I have the opportunity, if possible, to set things right. *So Mote It Be.*

CPSIA information can be obtained at www.ICGtesting.com
Printed in the USA
BVOW03s1856160913

331322BV00002B/159/P